I0151522

"Don't Fix It! Don't Force It! Just Flush It!"

A No Holds Barred Self-Help Guide to Eliminate Toxic Relationships

By:
CJ Hornes

LCCN 2017914223
ISBN 978-0-692-03406-4

 Phone: 678-814-3358
Email: hornescj@gmail.com
Website: www.cjhornes.com

I have tried to recreate events, locales, and conversations from my memories of them. To maintain their anonymity in some instances, I have changed the names of individuals and places; I may have changed some identifying characteristics and details such as physical properties, occupations and places of residence.

I'm not a medical doctor, and I do not make any claims of curing, healing or treating any illness. All rights are reserved 2017, and before using any information attained from this book, please consult a physician or therapist.

Illustrations by Paul Athol

Printed in the USA

CJ Hornes is a Certified Anger Management Facilitator trained by Anderson & Anderson Psychological Services, and she is also a Certified Emotional Intelligence Coach and Personal Development Specialist. Unashamed to use her life experiences as a teaching mechanism, she openly shares her life with anyone that will listen. In 2011, she founded Truth Outreach Center a 501 c3 non-profit organization that provides resources for homeless veterans, survivors of domestic violence and ex-offenders. Her other works include "21 Days to Renew the Mindset (Recovery & Redemption)" a curriculum created to help reduce recidivism.

To book CJ Hornes for speaking engagements or coaching services email hornescj@gmail.com or visit www.cjhornes.com

Table of Contents

Preface 7

Introduction 10

Fix Mr. Insecure 14

Fix the Functioning Alcoholic............................... 18

Fix the Leach 25

Force the Profit 27

Force the Pervert 31

Force the Controller 36

Fix the Pill Popper 46

The Devil in the Flesh 49

My No Self-Esteem Journal 53

Encouragement 89

Defining "You"..90

Low Self-Esteem...91

Life Balancing and Well-Being............................. 93

Verbal Abuse 99

"I Can Make You Love Me" 100

Definitions 108

Plan of Action 111

Detoxing From the Inside Out 112

Resources... 114

In loving memory of my mother "Ruby."

I can still hear you saying, "Lisa don't be letting that man hit on you."

Acknowledgements

To my son Raja

Whose strength has continuously supported me

And whose prayers have encouraged me.

Thank you, Son, I love you beyond words.

To my husband Rodney, aka "The Prosecutor," who

once said, "Your money is in your mouth,"

I love you immensely.

Thank you!

To my best friend Louvinia Cole, thank you for all your

prayers and support. Love is truly an action word.

Preface

An easy part of my book where I can give credit where it is rightfully due. I've been told that people come into your life for a season, reason, or lifetime, and it's up to us to be a good judge of character and recognize who's in it for the long haul, who served as a purpose or who's just for the moment.

I want to personally thank the people that came into my life for a brief second. I appreciate being lied to, dumped, cheated on, mentally, physically, and verbally abused. Oh, umm! I almost forgot to thank you for using me, wasting my time, shattering my self-esteem, and making me feel as if I was worthless.

EEEERRRRRRRRRRRR! Stop hold up…. Not! I wish I would consider thanking any of you for being nothing more than a 30-second tragic thought!

You caught me off my square during a weak moment in my life when I didn't know who I was or who's I was. I didn't know my worth, but I grew from every heartache and painful teardrop.

TOXIC

Adjective | tox·ic | \ˈtäk-sik\

Containing or being poisonous material especially when capable of causing death or serious debilitation •toxic waste •a toxic radioactive gas exhibiting symptoms of infection or toxicosis

Extremely harsh, malicious, or harmful •toxic sarcasm

Relating to or being an asset that has lost so much value that it cannot be sold on the market.

"Toxic." Merriam-Webster.com, Merriam-Webster, www.merriam-webster.com/dictionary/toxic. Accessed 2017.

Introduction

Over the years I've seen many amazing women succumb to being misused and abused while being in toxic relationships. The aftermath of physical abuse, verbal abuse, mental & emotional abuse, and even sexual abuse can lead to extremely low self-esteem and low self-worth. All of which ultimately affect your overall quality of life.

I wrote this book and enclosed actual excerpts from my journals with the hopes that it would enlighten and motivate you to make wiser choices and better decisions when it comes to dating and relationships.

Queen, you are the prize.

So what

exactly does it

mean to

flush-it???

Ask CJ

Many of you may think that shit is a derogatory word or a vulgar way to speak regarding fecal matter or having a bowel movement. After researching, I found out that shit is an adjective that describes waste, garbage, and toxins. Shit comes in many different forms, her shit, his shit, their shit, and plain old bullshit, and it's up to you to decide if you want to take any of the shit mentioned previously. Question for you, "When you can't have a bowel movement what do you do?"

If you're like most of us you either opt to take a laxative or herbal supplement, have a glass of prune juice, or get a colonic. Whatever, your preference is it all leads to the same outcome the same results in the toilet and what do you do? Flush it! Because if you don't, the buildup of toxins can be poisonous and cause you to have a variety of issues from psychological problems to physical problems that can even kill you. The same is true of relationships. You can't continue living the swine life—you know, rolling around in shit all day and night and loving it. Take a good, tough piece of toilet paper like Scott's and wipe the "I'm sorry," "I didn't mean to do it," "I won't do it anymore," and the "But I love you" right out your life! I can hear toilets flushing all over the world and clean up any residue with a good baby wipe!! A good clean start there's nothing like it.

"Insecure"

Mary, a beautiful young woman with three small boys, lives with her boyfriend, Earl. Earl seems to be a pretty decent guy. He's a short, chubby nerd who wears cheap gold-rimmed glasses and isn't that attractive. Since Mary is a beauty, you'd think he'd worship the ground she walks on, but just the opposite is true. No one would know from looking at Mary that she's a crack addict who had told me a gruesome tale of not having the money to get high and a local drug dealer made her have sex with a dog (a pit bull). An unfortunate but realistic truth. A story of low self-worth and perhaps the reason Earl was able to land a gem like Mary. I'm trying to figure it out and haven't been able to yet.

Well, there could be a good reason. Mary's family is filthy rich. Rich and beautiful. I'm certain that's the reason Earl hooked up with her? Mary's family owns one of the largest megachurches in the country. With her rare beauty and networking capabilities, she could easily have any man she wants. So, what's her problem? Why has she settled for an unattractive, short, no physique having guy with nothing going for himself? Mary has often confided in her girlfriends about Earl's abuse and his need to have a platform. Earl has even tried to get Mary to have sex with professional athletes for money telling her that she needed to take one for the team.

One day, Mary got home late, and Earl accused her of cheating. Who knows whether or not he had ever cheated on her before, but that didn't matter to him. What mattered was that she had cheated on him and he would teach her a lesson! He proceeded to call her every vulgar name in the book as she stood there trying to explain her whereabouts. Then, he grabbed her by her hair, threw her to the floor, and dunked her head in a bucket of mop water that contained pine-sol. Pine-sol should not be swallowed and is toxic and extremely poisonous. The main ingredient decreases motor function, slows respiration, and will lower your level of consciousness. Well, you can be sure that Earl didn't give a damn about that. His woman had cheated on him.

"You're a nasty whore!" He screamed at her. "I'll get you clean!"

Earl is very insecure and doesn't believe that Mary is out getting high, so when she gets home, he beats her. The very last time, he went even further and took a hammer and knocked all of her front teeth out! Why should she put up with a bastard like Earl? Guess what? She shouldn't. What should she do?

She should flush him, and she should flush the crack too. What is she doing with her life other than messing it up? Crack and Earl are both addictions, and she needs to get rid of both of them and start taking care of Mary!

Mary has the love and support of a God-fearing family.

Now all she needs to do is give a damn about herself and

get rid of the trash that's turning her life into garbage.

Mary has to learn how to start loving herself.

But how? What would you do differently?

_____

_____

_____

_____

_____

_____

_____

"The Functioning Alcoholic"

Tammy and Jeff look to be the perfect couple, and everyone loves them. But things were going on behind closed doors that no one else knew about.

As an investment banker, Tammy makes the most money in the home, and Jeff works a seasonal construction job. That means he has it easy. They have one child together, and Tammy has a child from a previous relationship. When Jeff is not working, he stays drunk for days—I guess you would call him a binge drinker. While Tammy's out working and earning money, he gets shit faced drunk. Nice, huh?

The kids constantly either find Jeff passed out on the floor or with his face lying in a plate of spaghetti. Guess he likes Italian food. It isn't good for the kids to see their step-father drunk and passed out, but it's obvious he doesn't give a crap about them. Jeff also becomes violent when he's drunk and lashes out at Tammy when she tries to stop him from drinking. She's trying to help him, but he doesn't appreciate it. So, why should she keep putting up with his shit?

Jeff's drinking is beginning to have an effect on Tammy at her job. She has been written up twice, and she's on the verge of losing her job. That would be bad for the family because she's the breadwinner. It would be bad for Jeff because he wouldn't have money to buy booze anymore. It's hard for Tammy to concentrate on doing her work when she has to run home at lunchtime to make sure everything is OK. Tammy has tried to get him help, but he's in denial, and so is his family. Jeff seems to think that he has it all together because he only drinks when he's off work. He has nothing together. He's a drunken idiot who's taking his problems out on a woman who's trying to help him. He needs help, but that isn't her responsibility.

What should she do? Some people might disagree with me on this one I'm sure…FLUSH-IT!

Jeff is what we call a functioning alcoholic. The trouble is, a functioning alcoholic still drags the people around them down with them. He goes to work, comes home, enjoys his family and friends, and looks the part of a perfect mate, but he's not. Jeff is not only doing great harm to himself but also to Tammy and her children, which they don't deserve. The kids deserve to grow up in a safe house, and Tammy deserves a man who treats her well. The relationship is not a healthy relationship, and you can't make Jeff get help, he has to want it for himself. In the meantime, send him packing! That's right, send him packing! Tammy should throw his shit out on the street before he hurts her or one of the kids. If she doesn't want to go down the drain with this abusive alcoholic, she needs to send him packing!

THE FUNCTIONING ALCOHOLIC

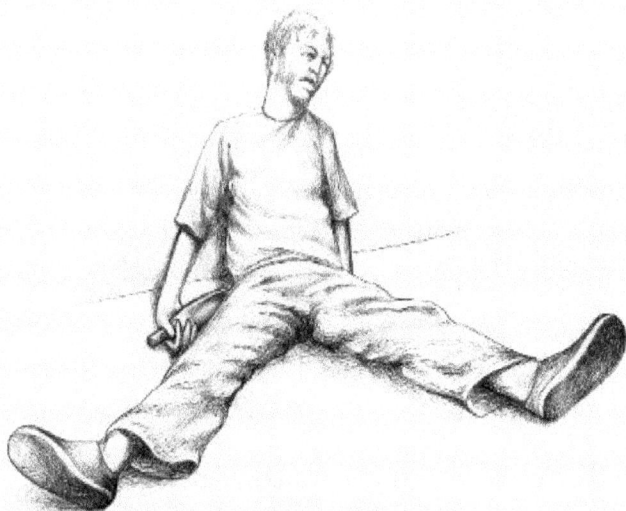

Ask CJ

As women, we are born natural nurturers, and we spend a lot of time trying to fix things, especially other humans. Many of us seek to fix other humans so that our relationships with them will be the way we want them to be, Whether it's fixing our man or spouse, fixing our friends, or fixing our children. We daydream about having the perfect relationships, if we can just get him to do this or be like that, then everything would be fine. No, it won't! You can't change anyone unless they want to change. Maybe you want him to be a certain way, but he's happy the way he is or could it be that he doesn't know that he even has a problem. So, all you're doing is wasting your time.

While you're fixing him and fixing other people you think need fixing, life goes on. He keeps living his life the way

22

he wants and doesn't give a damn what you think. He might even shit all over you if you allow him to. We have to get "IT," this thing called "LIFE"! We can no longer continue to play the victim because it becomes "allowed behavior." By allowing this behavior, you are no longer the victim,

You're the enabler.

Allowed Behavior is a behavior pattern that has been accepted and allowed to persist continuously due to learned helplessness or low self-esteem.

An enabler is a person that co-signs for negative allowed behavior. *"I support your mistreatment of me."*

Learned Helplessness occurs when you feel that you are no longer in control of a situation, so you give up and go along with the situation that you're allowing. Not realizing that you have the power to change the situation if you wanted to but fear and failure has deceived you into thinking that you can't.

"Leech"

John, a 27-year-old man, and Marie, a 28-year-old woman, have been living together on and off for seven years. John is currently in between jobs, and Marie works full-time days as a receptionist and goes to school part-time twice a week in the evenings. John and Marie are constantly fighting because he parties a lot with his friends, and he's never home. When he is at home, he usually sleeps all day instead of looking for a job. Should we call John a lazy slob? He certainly doesn't care that Marie pays all the bills, buys all the food, and puts gas in both vehicles. She also gives John money, so he's not broke all the time. What makes her think that's something she has to do? John feels that he is a young man and that he has plenty of time to look for a job and go to school and wishes Marie would stop nagging him about a job!

Ask CJ

What should Marie do? She should do just the opposite of what she's doing now. She should kick his ass to the curb. Where does John get off getting drunk every night and sleeping all day while Marie works days and goes to school at night? What the hell is that all about? He's a lazy slob.

Marie should flush this turd so fast that he breaks in half going down the toilet!

Here's why John is apparently not on the same page as Marie, and he has no interest in improving his current situation. He is using Marie not only to support him but also support his lifestyle in the streets. If he likes the street so much he ought to go live there! The rent is cheap.

Marie should get smart, take a day off from work and pack all of Mr. Man's personal belongings and set them outside, have her locks changed, and if necessary place a restraining order on the lazy bum!

"Prophet vs. Profit"

Her Excellency, Dr. Rev. Prophetess Jennifer had been single for a while because all of her time was being spent with religion. When Jennifer wasn't at church, she was either on the road preaching, at home studying the Bible or spending time in prayer. So when the slue-footed demon dog walked into her life, she was caught off guard. Shawn was a musician who pretended to be caught up in religion just to bamboozle her out of her money. After a short courtship, the two married, and that's when Jennifer begin to see Shawn's true colors. He ran all her credit cards up, he didn't pay any bills, he wanted his face on all flyers and advertisements that pertained to her ministry, and he didn't have any money he was broke. Shawn even went as far as to grab Jennifer by her throat during an argument. After being married a month or so, a mysterious call came for Jennifer from an unknown woman informing her that her new husband was married four previous times and that he had fathered five children. Five children that he does not take care of by five different women. Jennifer was outraged and didn't know what to do. Because she had been raised to believe that once you're married, you have to stay married, Jennifer felt as if she had let God and her family down she was so confused and heartbroken. It seems as if Shawn had a hidden agenda: he didn't want the Prophet, he wanted to profit. Fix it, Force it, or Flush it. Jennifer better flush this turd quick. He is a user, and he's out for self and self only. This piece of crap is looking for a free ride and a platform. Jennifer has to pick herself back up and realize we all make mistakes and we have all been deceived or lied to at some point in our lives.

Ask CJ

We try to fix him because he pays the bills and he's a good provider! We try to fix, fix, fix, fix, instead of flushing it and moving on. Learn from it, move on, and figure out what you got out of the experience.

I remember my aunt saying, "Lisa you have to be mindful of who you invite into your life for the rest of your life." I never really knew what she meant until I became pregnant by an abuser. I had invited a monster into my life for at least 18 years. What had I done? This is what happens when we don't get to know a person before engaging in sexual activity with them. Once you are physically intimate, you end up with distorted vision. Good sex with the wrong dude will mess your mind completely up. I mean you will find yourself co-signing for cars, buying clothes, sponsoring trips, bagging up dope, and being abused all at the same time. But because the pipe is laid right, you ignore the cuss outs and the controlling behavior in the beginning. After a while, the true colors of an abuser will

29

completely surface. Slaps, arm grabbing, telling you where you can and can't go, secluding you from your friends and family, name calling; bitch, hoe, etc., put-downs; you ain't shit, you stupid, you don't do shit, etc. I can remember an argument with one of my exes he called me a gutter carp! For years, I had no idea what a gutter carp was, but come to find out a carp is a nasty fish. Isn't that some shit?

"The Pervert"

Tiffany is fourteen and lives with her mom, Donna, and her mom's boyfriend, Richard. Richard is your average everyday piece of shit. Tiffany is an honor student and is growing into a very pretty young lady, which is something Richard has noticed. He's a pig and ready to bounce on this innocent young girl. Richard makes a sick slurping snake-like noise every time Tiffany walks by him to the point, where she hates to get up when he's in the same room with her. Why does this girl who's still a child, have to put up with this crap? Richard belongs on a sex offender list.

One night while Tiffany was in bed, she overheard a conversation between Richard and her mom,

"Why are Tiffany's little titties growing?" he asked.

The only response her mom gave was, "I don't know."

Tiffany couldn't believe what she was hearing. Why were they discussing her breasts? Richard was a disgusting pig, and she wished her mother would throw him out. A few weeks passed. One night, Tiffany was in bed asleep when she felt someone tugging at her thighs. She immediately pressed her thighs together as hard as she could. She hoped it would stop, but it didn't.

"Tiffany, open your legs," he said. It was her mom's boyfriend, Richard.

Tugging and pulling at her, but she didn't move. She pretended to be sleep and pressed her thighs together even tighter until he gave up and left, but Tiffany lay there crying and frightened, not knowing what to do. Why was this happening to her? She had never done anything to encourage Richard. He was a pig, and she hated him. He would be sorry if he ever came near her again!

Tiffany had a horrible day at school, thinking about that man touching her and wondering if she should tell her mom or not, and if she would get in trouble. The day was long, and Tiffany dreaded going home. She knew what Richard had done was wrong, but she didn't know what her mother's reaction would be. It wasn't the kind of thing a fourteen-year-old girl should have to deal with, and it was all Richard's fault.

When Tiffany got home, her mom was cooking dinner. She put her book bag down and told her mom that she needed to tell her something.

"Yeah, what is it?" Her mom asked.

Tiffany didn't quite know how to put it, so she said, "I think somebody was in my room last night rubbing on my leg." Her mother said,

"Are you sure?"

That was all Tiffany heard, the rest of the conversation was a blur.

The conversation never came up again but, but now her mom treated her differently. She was meaner, and she even snatched Tiffany out the top bunk in the middle of the night, asking her what had she been doing in here. Tiffany screamed and cried.

"What are you talking about?" she asked her mother.

Apparently, Richard had been out of bed for a while, so her mom automatically thought he was in her room. This behavior went on until Tiffany started to tell teachers and friends what was going on. Social services got involved, and Tiffany found herself in a doctor's office being examined and all she remembers is a very painful uncomfortable feeling.

Tiffany and her mom went to court, and the court declared Tiffany, a liar. Apparently, the doctor's report showed that Tiffany was still a virgin and nobody had touched her. The judge ordered a psychological evaluation and for Tiffany to start counseling. He informed Tiffany that if she ever ran away again, they would put her in a girl's home. The social worker on the case told Tiffany to do as her mom and stepdad told her, even if he told her to get his slippers, "you must get them." Tiffany was hurt, and she found herself hating her mom. She knew she had told the truth and her mother should have believed her. Was there anyone she could trust?

Eventually, Tiffany ran away to another state.

What should have been done here? A young lady with no one on her side, not even her mom. The mom should not have doubted her daughter, and she should have confronted the boyfriend and called the police instead of blaming the child. The mother allowed her boyfriend to abuse her child and that was wrong. No matter how you look at it, it was wrong. Tiffany took the blame and eventually ran away from home.

*Child Molesting is a form of child abuse defined as the act of sexually touching a child who is 14 years of age or younger.

Studies have shown that 1 in 5 girls and 1 in 20 boys are victims of child sexual abuse.

Child molesters usually know their victims and can be close friends or relatives.

1-888-PREVENT

"The Controller"

Danny and Nicole have been together since they were teenagers. Danny is a local drug dealer, and Nicole works at the bank. Danny was raised by his adoptive parents and had a pretty decent upbringing. His adoptive parents were Pastors at the local church and provided their kids with all the desires of their heart. On the other hand, Nicole grew up in an abusive home with her mom and stepdad who fought all the time. Nicole even remembers trying to help her mom, but she ended up with her first black eye at the age of thirteen.

Nicole and Danny have been together for six or seven years, and they fight all the time, mostly because Danny is very jealous and controlling. The relationship has been a nightmare. So why do they stay together? Danny has even gone as far as to chase Nicole into her job and slam her against the wall. It just so happened that Nicole's supervisor walked out in the nick of time, saving her from a fight. On Nicole's 25th birthday, Danny told Nicole that he didn't want strippers at her birthday party, but Nicole wanted strippers, so she ordered strippers. After all, it's her party, and she could do whatever she wanted to do she was turning 25.

On the night of the party, Danny had no idea that strippers would be there. When he saw the strippers, he acted a fool in front of everybody. People tried to get him to calm down, but he felt disrespected and was not having it. The party ended early, and Nicole took most of her birthday cake home, but before she could get the cake to their apartment, Danny knocked the cake and Nicole down the stairs. When Nicole got up, she had cake all over her dress and Danny grabbed her, placing her head between his legs. He started beating her on the top of her head with his fist, and she couldn't get away as he continued to pound blows to the back of her neck and head. Her downstairs neighbor came out screaming, "stop yall... stop let her go," and he finally let her go.

The next day everything was back to normal as if nothing had happened.

A few weeks later, Danny told Nicole that she couldn't go out to the club with her cousins… but, he was going out with his boys. Nicole decided that she was going out too so she had her cousin circle back and picked her up. When Nicole walked through the door of her apartment, Danny short jabbed her in the eye, and it closed shut. Nicole couldn't see a thing, and her entire face and head was in pain. What was she going to do about work on Monday? Nicole didn't have any more personal days at work and knew that the bank would fire her if she called in so she had to go to the bank in person so that they could see she had an emergency situation. Danny drove Nicole to her job. Nicole's supervisor looked at her and said, "You don't have to take that, you know, we can get you some help." But Nicole didn't want help because this was normal. Growing up, she had seen her dad throw hot rice on her mom when she was only three years old. And her mom and stepdad did this all the time, but they stayed together, and her mom had never involved the police or any outside influences in her relationship's that was a no-no. Danny initiated sex that night and pulled Nicole on top

38

of him, Nicole rode Danny till he came and she made sure the lights stayed on because she wanted him to see what he had done to her; she wanted him to see her pain. But Danny showed no signs of emotion or concern.

Nicole had to be off work until her eye opened up and she was able to see. Nicole thought if they moved out of the neighborhood that they currently lived in her and Danny would have a better relationship. But they didn't, and the fighting continued.

One day, Nicole told him that she wanted out of the relationship. She was tired of the cheating and the beatings. To her surprise, Danny said, "Let's talk." But Nicole was tired of talking and fighting. Danny grabbed Nicole and spit in her face. Nicole couldn't believe what he had done. There was thick spit running down her face; she wiped it off with her hand. She was disgusted with his behavior.

She looked at Danny. "I still don't want to be with you anymore," she said.

Danny then spit in Nicole's face again but this time hawking greenish, yellow snot like mucus that streamed down her face and she almost threw up but, she didn't. There was a box cutter on the couch that the cable man had used earlier in the day. Nicole grabbed the box cutter and ran at Danny screaming and yelling, "Spit goes in your mouth you nasty Motherfucker," while slicing at his face, but he threw his arms up to block the cuts. It didn't matter. Nicole went at him, full speed, completely zoned out—she had snapped. After hearing the screams, she stopped. Danny looked at her in shock as he took off his rain jacket. Nicole had never seen so much blood it shot out like a sprinkler system, and he fell to the floor. Nicole walked into the kitchen, grabbed some ice, glass, a bottle of Hennessey, and poured herself a drink. She then walked off leaving him to bleed out on the floor. Nicole had changed her mind; she was tired of taking abuse.

This whole situation could have been avoided at the first sign of abuse, which in his case was his controlling behavior. Danny should have been flushed a long time ago. But Nicole had grown up like this, and no one had ever told her any different. She thought it was normal to argue and fight with your boyfriend and then pretend that everything is OK.

POWER....YOU HAVE THE POWER TO MOVE FORWARD. YOU WERE BORN GREAT, AND THERE'S NOTHING THAT A TOXIC PERSON CAN DO ABOUT IT. THEY WANT YOUR POWER! DON'T GIVE AWAY YOUR POWER AND IF YOU'VE GIVEN YOUR POWER AWAY TAKE IT BACK!

Ask CJ

You need to – and you can – learn to stand up for yourself. Your life has more value than giving it away to some two-bit asshole.

Once you have been screwed over by someone, you should never….ever allow them to do it again. If you do, you are an idiot. Do not put yourself back in that same position or predicament again because if you do people will continue to screw you around. You have to learn how to take better care of yourself. It is very important that you learn how to love yourself. If you don't know how to love yourself, how can anyone else love you properly? You have no idea what love looks like. I can remember being forced to have sex right after I had an abortion. My boyfriend at the time was a jerk, but I didn't know that he was selfish and didn't care about me at all. But at that time, I couldn't have cared about myself either. I didn't know any better.

I had to learn the hard way. Local jokers look better going than they did coming. There are a lot of single women as well as women in relationships today, so I want to say this to you right now... are you listening? Don't marry just anybody to say you have a husband. Don't date just anybody to say you have a man. You do not have to settle for less. Have higher expectations of yourself and know your worth. If another human is mentally, physically, emotionally or sexually abusing you, then they don't love you, point blank, simple! I don't care if it's momma, daddy, uncle, aunt, brother, sister, husband, wife, boyfriend, girlfriend, teacher, preacher, pastor. Whomever! Get rid of them because they don't love you! And if they do love you, they don't love you on the level that you need to be loved! It's not the kind of love that you want in your life.

Don't Fix It! Don't Force It! Just FLUSH-IT! Do not accept the bullshit! We all have some form of shit in our lives, and we don't know what to do with it. Shit comes in many different forms, and it can originate from a variety of places. We accept things because we think we have to, we don't know any better, or we've been misinformed, misguided, and somewhat ignorant. Ignorant is not necessarily a bad thing. The dictionary defines it simply as a lack of knowledge. But, now you KNOW! Not everyone is required to be a part of your life or in your life forever. God does not permit people to mistreat you. You permit people to abuse you. It's called allowed behavior, and it starts with self. Respect yourself enough to let people go. You need to know and understand that you deserve the best. People will abuse and take advantage of you if you don't understand that. You deserve the best life and the best relationship however, the best isn't some jackass who abuses you mentally, physically, emotionally or sexually all while claiming to love you.

Society has turned us into professional fixers. We spend the majority of our lives trying to fix relationships instead of letting go of the crap in our lives! We try to fix him because we don't want to be alone! We love him so much, he's my kids' dad, we have history, I can't see myself without him, and I can't see myself with anyone else. We don't realize that we'd be better off alone rather than staying with an abusive piece of shit! We try to fix him because we see the good in him! We try to fix him for so many reasons, and when the fixing doesn't work, we force it. We force it until we become broken into so many pieces that we now need fixing.

"Pill Popping"

Renee and Charles are married and have no children. Renee is a successful businesswoman who works in education and is not only smart but also poised and polished. She's a well put together woman that any man should be proud to have by his side. She has been lucky career-wise and is very successful. But when it comes to men it's a different story. Renee has been married three times, which makes Charles hubby number four. Each husband has had major issues; however, this one is the worst of them all. This fool is a pill-popping pharmaceutical druggy who doesn't work or pay bills. He just lays on his ass all day in a drugged stupor while collecting SSI. But the money he collects isn't enough to support his drug habit. Charles went to Renee's job to harass her for money so he could get high. That must have been very humiliating for her. Unfortunately, it got a lot worse because he had his drug dealer with him! Charles owed the dealer a lot of money, and like the absolute moron he

47

was, he told the guy that his wife had the money with her at

work.

Ask CJ

What should she do?

Flush him and the entire situation down the drain. Renee is putting her life as well as her career in danger. I mean is there any question? If she stayed with him, she might not survive. Charles is an idiot, and he's dangerous. Only a moron would tell a drug dealer that someone has his money when they don't. Obviously, by doing this, he has proved that he doesn't give a fuck about Renee.

She needs to GET RID OF THIS CREEP and fast. She's successful, and he doesn't know his ass from his elbow. She should throw him out on the street so he can figure out how to survive on his own, then maybe he might appreciate everything she did for him. Or maybe he can move in with his drug dealer.

"The Devil in the Flesh"

Janice was my neighbor, and we lived in a duplex. I stayed upstairs, and she stayed downstairs for a couple of years, so I witnessed her and her husband fighting from time to time, and she'd witnessed my boyfriend and me fighting. I remember my boyfriend and I had broken up, but he was still stopping by my house and still coming by and parking down the street stalking me. So on this one particular night, I came home from a date, and there were police cars, and fire trucks everywhere and my house was taped off—I had no idea what had happened. When they finally let me and my date through the yellow tape, we were able to go upstairs. My date and I were sitting on the couch and all of a sudden, the closet door opens, and it's my ex. He had been hiding in the closet listening to our conversation the entire time while the police were downstairs. So I'm sitting there scared because my date has a gun and my ex-has a gun. Just to keep the peace, I asked my date to leave. I remember him saying, "Are you sure?" I'm like "yeah, I'm sure; I'll be fine." So my date left, and my ex immediately wanted to know who my date was and was I fucking him. I asked him was he crazy and how did he get in my house. And why were the police there and what happened to Janice, my downstairs neighbor? He told me that Janice and her husband Ricky were fighting and that he heard the entire fight. He told me that it started in their living room and ended in the bathroom. What happened was her husband had doused her with rubbing alcohol and threw a match on her and set her on fire; her whole body was engulfed in flames. Seeing that she was on fire, her husband tried to put her out by pushing her into the shower. So I asked my ex, "You said you heard this whole thing, but you didn't try to go help her?" His response is bone chilling... "It's not my business." I'm in total awe at this moment. I'm thinking to myself how could you stand by and listen to a woman being beaten and do nothing? To hear her being set on fire and do nothing! My ex- went on to say that he heard Janice begging and pleading with her husband "please...NO! Don't do this to me!"

Janice was in the hospital for months with third-degree burns covering her face, arms, and breast area. When she came home I couldn't bring myself to tell her that there was a witness that heard the entire dreadful and barbaric act, but even more disheartening was the simple fact that Janice was on Ricky's visitation list at the prison.

I see a pattern of abuse here. It seems that Janice had become accustomed to the cycle of abuse. It was normal for Ricky and her to fight, fuss, and cuss, then makeup and act as if nothing happened.

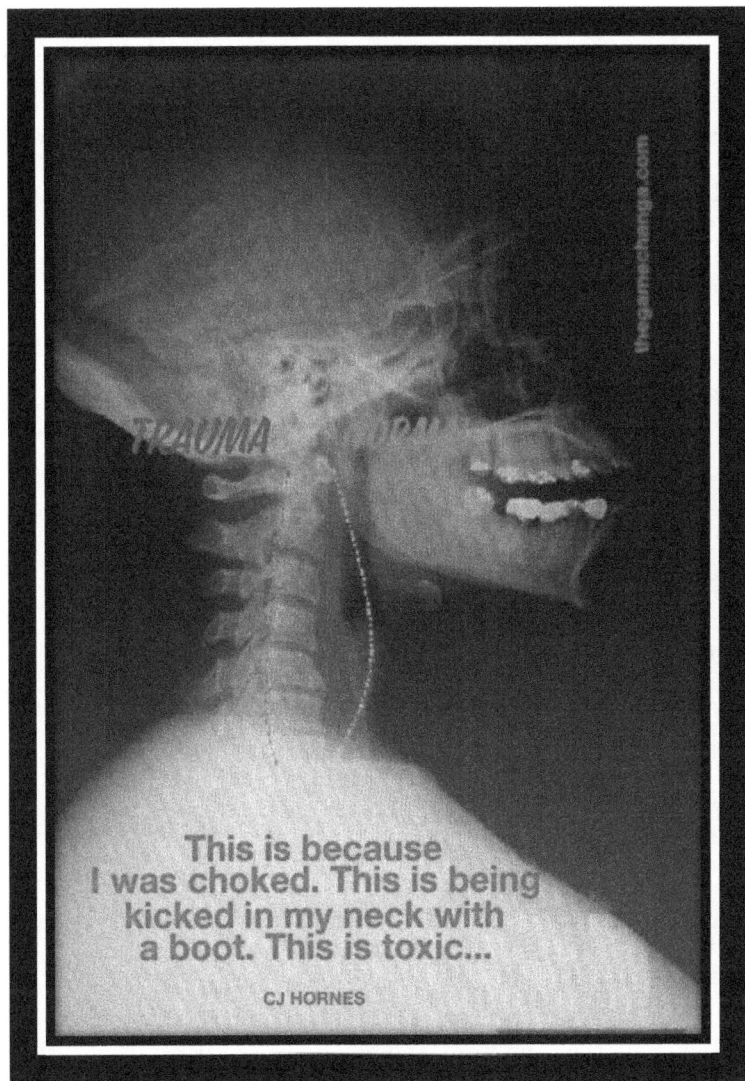

This is because
I was choked. This is being
kicked in my neck with
a boot. This is toxic...

CJ HORNES

"My No Self-Esteem Journal"

August 2, 2005

I feel that I am a woman somewhat where I want to be, but not exactly. I know I want something more, but I still have to figure out what that is. I'm not where I want to be, but this is the road to it. Or at least that was what I thought at the time. Later, I would learn I was wrong and wanted something more.

Writing this journal is my way of telling you a little about me. I'm a 32-year-old mother of two. I had babies by two worthless pieces of shit. Well, I guess they all are huh? Maybe not all, but most of them. The two that I messed with certainly were.

I'm engaged to a man with 10-20 personalities. You could say he's out of his fucking mind. One of them is kind, sweet, talkative, and very gentle, but the other nine are crazy motherfuckers. I'm not too sure about him anyway. I will tell you the rest later. A little at a time is more than enough.

I picked up my fiancé from work, and he's depressed as usual for some odd reason. I know that he hates his job, sometimes

I feel sorry for him. Silence in the truck… I need to keep my sanity. It's a thing that's kind of important to me.

August 3, 2005

So here goes another messed up day! Just another day in my life similar to the other 364 in a year. Why am I putting up with this crap? I deserve better than to spend my life with a crazy bastard. This man ignores me all the time. All he does is watch TV, suck his thumb, and ask me to suck his dick every morning. Then, he sends me on a liquor run. This happens every damn day! He's a big fan of having his body parts getting sucked. He sucks his thumb, and he wants me to blow him. Well, it may be fun for him, but I'm exhausted! Frankly, I wish he'd find someone else for his morning blow job.

I told him that I didn't want to have another heated fight with him. I also told him that he was ugly and he told me to shut my fat ass up! Have you ever known a more

loving couple? He really hurt my feelings because he's never called me fat before. I'm not fat! He's a stupid asshole! Now that I know how he feels there will not be a wedding. I'll be damned if I'll marry anyone who treats me the way this crazy fool does.

Enhancement is not a necessity. I don't want to need a man. I want him to need me. But this fool has no idea what he needs because he's so damn drunk all the time. Maybe if he sobered up a little, we could get somewhere...

(Later)

He's sloppy drunk again. So guess what? We had another fight! Last time, he hit me in my back so hard that I couldn't scream. I just laid there in dead silence as the tears rolled down my face. The pain was unbearable. I have to figure out why I put up with this shit. I deserve a lot better.

He cursed me so badly—bitch, hoe, whore! His true self-exploded. He told me that he's the creator of shit and that I'm nothing... He fought me until I called my son and told him I was scared. He told me that he'd kill me, that he would bust my head into the concrete. God help me! I can't marry this man.

56

He needs help. I'm sad. I need help too! Why do I always end up with men that beat women?

August 4, 2005

Today same ole same ole! It never changes, but I need to realize that I'm the only one who can change things. He certainly isn't going to. I went to work. Before I did, we argued. He is a trip for real! I went to K & G and bought myself a cute bag, and it made me feel better.

I'm feeling down; him calling me fat blew me away. I thought he liked my body. I'm hurt, but it's ok. I'll be working on me from now on. I refuse to see myself as a slave anymore.

August 6, 2005

Well, I met his folks from New York today, and of course, he acted a fool. He fought my sister and me. My neck is red. He is crazy. I guess, what they say is true a drunk ain't shit. I can't take any more. He needs to be alone. I'm serious. I'm moving, or he's moving. One or the other!

August 7, 2005

Today, we had sex for the first time in 3 days. It's crazy. It wasn't good nor was it bad. I was just there! I'm so sad at this point in my life. I deserve so much more. I feel like this is a recap of the nine years that I spent with my ex when I was an ignorant girl, fresh out of Mississippi. No one ever showed me any love. All I ever knew was abuse. I watched my mother get beat all the time, and she'd sit there like it was nothing! Oh, how I hated her boyfriend for hurting her. He was lower than shit. Now, I'm in the same shape. I hate my ex, my daughter's father. I never wanted his child. That's probably why I'm so hard on my daughter. God, please help me to understand what's going on inside my glass house. I try to understand what's going on. I give of myself all the time. I'm loyal and don't understand why I have to go through so much.

God spoke to me while I was cleaning the prison bathroom. "Follow me, and I will give you everything you want." I was startled because I was the only one in the bathroom. I know I need to go to church and pray more. God, please help to bring me closer to you, to be more Christ-like and less me like... Increase in me so I can decrease.

August 9, 2005

You need to sit down for this one! My future husband told me that he is going to start working out from 12 a.m. until 1 a.m., every morning. Is he insane? Why would you leave your wife all night long? You be the judge. He's full of shit. He either is on something or full of himself. He needs to start realizing how crazy and selfish that is.

(Later)

He got home, we argued, and he told me that I couldn't go to the gym with him because I might see someone and start something,

"Who?" I asked. "What the hell is going on at work?"

"You don't know how to talk or act in a professional setting," he said.

What? This jack legged nigga got me pegged all wrong. Is he serious…? I guess, let me take my unprofessional, ignorant ass away then. How about that? He also said that he's moving. Ok. I like that.

August 10, 2005

Another day of alcohol and mayhem! I'm done arguing with him. He went over to our neighbor's house and drank for two hours. As long as he can smoke and drink, he's cool. I'm tired of this man. Oh, so tired! I've got to get rid of him somehow. I deserve better than this asshole. I just asked God to help me. If it can't get right, please remove everything that's stopping me from doing what I need to do for myself.

August 11, 2005

Today, I'm sad. I don't want him to be a knight in shining armor. I just want him to love me more than anything and anyone. I think he's cheating. It breaks my heart to think that he is, but I have to face the truth. Well, maybe it's the truth, and maybe it's all my imagination. I'll tell you more later.

August 14. 2005

He left the house at 8:30 am after drinking and partying all night to pick up the handyman, but he rode his bike???? He flipped his motorcycle, it drug him, and he ended up being hurt pretty badly. The problem was that he didn't want to go to the hospital, but I begged him to. We were there all night.

God help me. He broke his leg, and he might need surgery. They put a cast on him from his groin to his toes. He is in so much pain; I hate to see him in any pain. I feel sorry for him. I'll do all I can for him to make him comfy. I just hope he appreciates it, but I'm not sure he will. Things just have to get better because it's impossible for us to continue this way much longer.

August 15, 2005

The days are long and hard for us. He's in terrible pain. I gave him a sponge bath, and his breakfast, and spent the whole day with him. My poor baby, I love him, and it hurts me to see him suffer. I have to be stronger for him! He needs me, and that feels good.

August 16, 2005

He's irritable and ungrateful. I'm there 100%, and it's still not enough. He always wants more and gives so little. I had a feeling things would turn out this way, but I had hoped they wouldn't. I gave him everything I could, and all he did was complain that I wasn't giving him enough. What the fuck does he want? I didn't mind helping him because he needed me, but now I do mind.

Ungrateful BASTARD!!!

August 21, 2005

Are you there God? It's me. I'm tired. I drank all day. Things are not good at work or home. I need your help. My life is just too hard, and I need some help. Please don't ignore me; please listen to me.

I'm at a point where I feel like I have lost it. My nerves are bad, my right eye won't stop twitching, and my head hurts all the time. I can't take anymore. I'm fat, and I feel so unhappy. I hate the smell of smoke, but he smokes all day and won't stop smoking or slow down. He takes and takes from me and gives nothing. I help him even though he makes me so angry that I start yelling. The devil makes such a fool of him. I can't make him love me more or love himself. People have to want to change and marrying him won't change him, it will only make things worse.

September 3, 2005

I'm tired of writing depressing bullshit. This is highly insensitive, but I think he's a shitty ass, big face, and flat foot trifling ass nigga! I can keep going... I'm tired of him. I'm starting to feel like I did before slowly but surely! I have never met a bigger jerk. This man has mistreated women for a long time. He's a jerk, and I have never had low self-esteem or been hard up for a man. I'm dealing with a monster, a dirty low-down selfish dog. At what point do I live out my dreams. Fuck him! The headaches are back, the pain, the hate.

It's been a rough week. I've been degraded and fucked over long enough. This man told me that no matter where I get in life, I'll always be two levels beneath him, then he threw his crutches at me. Two levels beneath him would mean I was living underground. No way! I am better than he is. I don't deserve this, and I won't take it anymore. He can go to hell!

September 9, 2005

He's drunk again at 9:30 a.m. with his friend. I'm upset, so I decided to take his friend home. Maybe that will make him stop drinking for five minutes.

By the time I left for work, he was already drunk. I'm exhausted. This man has a problem, and I don't know what to do. He is angry at the world. We had one good day, and now everything is back to normal. I have so many ideas and no one to help me implement them. I feel like I'm alone. Talk to you later…. I'm one damn angry black woman. I've had enough, and I'm ready for a change.

September 13, 2005

This morning, he woke up and looked right at me.

"How do you know you love me?" He asked.

Doesn't he know that already? Why would he ask me such a thing? I put up with too damn much! Is this a ploy to keep from getting married next month? Well, we just decided to postpone the wedding again. He says that we shouldn't rush things and that he wants to enjoy the ceremony. Yeah, sure. I can't wait to see what he comes up with next.

December 6, 2005

Long time since I've written but here goes. My fiancée left me again, after 11 months of putting up with his shit. He has been gone ten days now. At first, I was all torn up; now I'm better. The longer he stays away, the better I'm able to come to grips with the situation. I have never been treated so badly. I deserve better and intend to find it for myself. Why shouldn't I? I know there's a man out there who'll treat me the way I should be treated, which isn't the way this drunken moron treats me.

I hope he stays in whatever gutter he's living in.

December 10, 2005

I talked to him all day and made a fool out of myself. I didn't want to, but I did. Never again! I've realized that we are finished. Fuck him and our relationship. I've put up with enough of his fucking crap, and I won't put up with anymore.

I'll give him back his ring soon as I can. With the next guy, I'll be more of a vulture and less of a lady. It'll be about all I can get, and I intend to get as much as I can. No one is ever going to make a fool of me again. I feel like I was used for the good, but oh well, life is the dash. I can't wait to move out of town. It will be a new start, a new beginning for me and my kids.

December 11, 2005

He's been missing for two days, no cell phone. I guess the phone is dead. He's probably laid up somewhere. Cool. Let him stay wherever he is as long as it's not with me.

December 14, 2005

I talked to him last night. He was out of it. He asked me to come and get him, but he gave me the wrong street information. I gave up and went home. Let him get his ass wherever he needs to be. He texted me and told me how much he needed and missed me. Then today, he tells me that this was my fault. Is he kidding? He said I was the reason he's in the shape he's in. It's easier to blame me than to take responsibility for himself. He cold-heartedly blamed me. He sounded drunk as hell! I'm really sad, but God is good all the time.

December 16, 2005

Today, I sent one of my guy friends to his momma's door. I was so happy to see him, my stomach dropped… But once he saw me, he ran in the house. I was devastated, but I must move on. I've done all I can for him. He has no faith, and I pity him. The longer he's gone, the easier it is for me. I didn't cry today, I prayed. I'm going shopping and to my cousin's birthday party. I want to have some fun!

December 19, 2005

Ugh! Another horrible day. When will it stop?

December 21, 2005

Lord help me! Please send him home! I need him to lead me.

December 22, 2005

Alone again! No, he didn't call. I finally stopped calling him. A friend came over. I think she's disgusting, and I can't believe I slept with her she had tissue crumbs in her butt.

December 25, 2005

It's 6:43 a.m. I woke up at 5. I can't sleep. It's been a month since he left so I asked myself a question: Do I want this man or do I just miss having someone around? I don't like a lot of things about him, so I'll list likes and dislikes. He loves his friends more than me, loves smoking more, doesn't believe in me, doesn't believe in Jesus, loves to impress people and gain community acceptance, and puts his family in his business. Is he the right man for me? I wonder. I think I should want something better for myself. Do I like myself enough to get what I want?

December 28, 2005

I finally put his pictures away. This is a pain far worse than any bullet. I can't imagine life without him. I can't stand feeling this way, but I have no choice. I have to get better. I know it will get better, but it will take time. I have to look to the future and not live in the past.

My hair is falling out, my weight is down, and my head hurts. I can't take anymore. I thought about suicide, but I don't want to go to hell! I'm sure that's where I'll go if I kill myself. I can't stop crying, and I sleep all day. These pills are killing me, slowly. My life took a turn for the worst. I'm so lost, so lost! I don't want this life. God, please help me. He is sick. I can't believe he's doing this. My nerves are bad. I need this to end.

Take the alcohol from his mind. God help him! God help both of us! Deliver him, Lord, please!

December 31, 2005

I'm alone on New Year's Eve. I miss him. I'm hurting. I now realize what I had... what others wanted? My life took a nose dive... I just tried to call. He won't answer. I miss him. I see what others saw in him, but now he's gone. I'm starting a new job next week, and I'm nervous. I need a break. I need something good in my life.

January 8, 2006

Today is our anniversary. I will be reminiscing all day. I'm not going to call him. I guess he likes living in Alabama. Good for him. I was hoping that we would work things out, but I guess we aren't going to. I just wanted him to slow down on the alcohol. Maybe I went about it the wrong way? I can only pray for him. He has to have a strong woman because he's weak. I still love him, but enough is enough. He hasn't become a whole man yet; he still thinks like a boy. My body is numb. I hate sleeping alone. Happy Anniversary to me. I'm tired of crying; I just need someone to love me regardless. God, please send me a good, loving, nurturing, God-fearing husband.

January 25, 2006

Well, I finally decided to write to him. It's been a long time. I went to the sticks of Alabama to get him and got my feelings smashed. He has a new woman. What a fucking bastard! She is eighteen and pregnant, so she says. He was drunk when I talked to him. I'm very hurt. What happened in the last two months of my life? I miss him. Hope she makes him happy. What happened to my life? I'm so hurt. God help me. I need to find a better life, a better man. A man who will treat me the way I deserve to be treated.

He can go to hell!!!

February 24, 2006

I will not write any more sorrow. I'm happy today. I've learned so much in one year. I'm in love for the first time. I've been celibate for three months. I miss him so, but in my heart, I believe that one day he'll come home. I pray for him every night. May God bless him. I've come a long way as a woman, lady, wife; I'm ready... Send him God.

July 3, 2006

"The sex was good. You had my mind, and I let you come back, every time, violated cross the line…. Always waited so patiently. Thinking that he was going to marry me…"

"I've done enough crying. Time to say bye-bye, do something for me." Yes Mary J. it sounds good until reality hit me.

July 6, 2006

So, he told me that I was not righteous, which is why he can't marry me. Wow! Are you kidding me? I was blown away…Who does the drunken moron think he is? I look like crap. As I sit and think and think and look back at everything, I've been a fool. I feel like crap. My self-esteem is about the size of a penny. How can you do so much for a man and he still feels that you're beneath him? I am saddened. I was never in love with my other kid's fathers, nor was I ever there for them like I am for this man. Why have I wasted so much time and energy on him? My soul hurts so badly. I have run and run and chased and looked for and took care of someone who doesn't give a damn if I'm breathing! Where is this love for me? It never existed. I never mattered to him at all. He told me to shove it. After he had broken his leg, I thought that we'd be closer than ever. Maybe that's what I wanted, but not him. I thought I had the chance to show him that I loved him no matter what, but it didn't work. He left me soon after the crutches were gone and started sleeping with someone else. The hurt and pain I feel will never leave because he's the same. I took my fool ass all the way to the swamps of Alabama for nothing. At what point do I get it? Am I afraid of being alone? Do I crave a love that bad that I continue to allow this man to walk all over me? There are no words… sometimes, I just want to die. All the cooking, cleaning, sexing, looking out for in the world won't change his opinion of me. It comes out when he's drunk. One thing I know is that I'll never take this kind of abuse from another man. NEVER!

I want to be the apple of my husband's eye, the love of his life. I want to be the most important thing in his life. I want

74

him to adore me and not be able to live without me. But this jerk doesn't care whether I live or die. Through the lonely nights, I let the enemy trick me into gambling away all of my money. I feel like a fool. I look like a fool. Hell, I am a fool, a fool for love. Life is about choices, and I continue to make the wrong choices over and over. When a person shows you who they are, believe them. I have to learn how to make the choices that are best for me.

I received a lick so hard to the temple that I thought that I was going to die. My shoulder is still out of place all because he wanted to drink and drive. I wonder what my mom would say. When she found out the other dude was hitting me, she called and told me, "Lisa don't be letting that man beat you!"

Shame on me. I'm smart enough to know that I shouldn't let him hit me. So, why do I put up with it?

I've spent about 15k on him since he has been back in my life and let's not talk about all the money I gave the casino trying to find comfort. I still don't have a car, and I neglected my bills... All dumb shit! That's so irresponsible. I should know better. Put your man first, and he'll keep you first. So, I thought. God, I don't think I'll ever love another, no matter how wonderful he is. I'll probably look over it... Like Derrick, he was so good to me. He would send for me, take me shopping, cared about my well-being, and paid my bills, even cared about my kids. His folks were great, really successful people. I dumped him because he had a small penis. Where was my logic? Dick doesn't make the man, now I know. The man loved me for me; he didn't try to change my hair or my personality. I lost out because two years after that, he got married and bought his wife a home in Virginia Beach... Now, I'm sitting here in the dark thinking about what my life would have been like. I can't live in the past; learn and press on. I'm 33 years young, and I've been through enough for two people's lives. I hide behind a façade. My life only seems good if no one knows what's going on.

I don't want to love anymore. I just want to be. I want to live my own life and find the things that make me happy. I thank God for sanctity because sometimes, I feel like I'm losing it. There has to be a better way, a better life. God, can I have a little happiness? I do too much. I've done too much. I want something better for myself. With your guidance, I will find it. Nothing or no one is going to stop me.

God send me someone who goes above and beyond pleasing me, someone who will go out of their way to prove to me that they are the one for me. I'm the prize. I'm the one they can't live with out. Send me a husband that fears you. A funny, respectful, loving and understanding man... a husband that's not confused. I want someone loyal who knows their place and understands mine. A man who knows what to say, what not to say, and someone who makes me feel good about myself. I'm not a bad person. I hurt no one, but I always get hurt. I have changed so many things about myself just to be a better person.

It's almost 10:00 p.m. I'm sure he won't come home... Oh well!

July 7, 2006

I caught him with a bitch… I couldn't see her face. He took off and jumped on the 45 interstate and just his luck, the police stopped me. So, I lost him.

It's over. I'm in love with someone else! Guess with whom? Me! Yep! I've fallen in love with myself, and I'll make myself the best person I can be. No one is going to stop me. I'll be the best me that I can be.

I packed all of his stuff and put it by the door, so there is no need for him to come in. It's a wrap. I sat here in the dark alone… I'll be alone, coward ass nigga!

Later~

Found him. Guess where? At his mom's. He had nothing to say. He said the woman that he was with was his sister. How much of a fool does he think I am? He's one big fat liar, but it's all good. He can have her. That's the last time he spends the night out on me… KARMA!

He said he's tired of arguing. I'm sick of his shit! Is he serious?

I hate my daughter's father worse than God hates sin, and I'm 90% fed up with this fool. This man does not love me. It's written all over him. Enough of this shit already.

July 10, 2006

Last night, I got drunk again. No reason why… I needed sex. It was drunken sex, but I had no other outlet. I begged him to stay sober. He said he would and that we would kick it when I get home from work, the next day.

July 11, 2006

No call, no answer, I assumed the worst….

I got home and yep, pissy drunk as usual. God help me.

July 21, 2006

Last night, he decided to leave. I'm sad, but that's his choice. I tried to stop him. I feel like a fool; I guess I make him unhappy, all the trying to make him happy has backfired. I've done too much, and it wasn't appreciated at all... I've learned, "let the man court you." Also, never go out your way to please anyone but God and your husband.

August 14, 2006

I had a long talk with him. He had few words, as usual. I don't think he believes me. He takes me for a joke. I'm so sincere about my life and where I want to be... We'll know real soon if he's to be a part of my future. I have a plan and an agenda, so let's see how this goes.

August 15, 2006

So, I asked him when are we going to get married? His usual response, "I don't know." So, I suggested next week. He told me that my attitude hasn't changed, that he hasn't seen a change in me. Oh my God! This mother-fucker has some nerve. I have sat here like a fool and pleased him over and over. Trying my best to make him happy and this is what I get, "nothing"? This fool has bumped his head, or I'm just that dumb to sit around and please a man. I give all of me—mentally, sexually, and financially. This month alone, I gave him plenty of money for his bills. Nobody else helps this motherfucker, and I'm tired of his excuses. I have to make a life-changing move. Fuck love. I got to do me. I love me, and it's time to show it. I could have so much. I look at all the time and money that I've put into this relationship in the last two years. What for I asked? Nothing! He doesn't understand what a union is… Wow! Just Wow!

November 8, 2006

After the pain and all that I have been through, I still can't explain… I asked myself, why did I want to marry this man? Is he wonderful, loving, caring, outgoing, spontaneous…the bomb in the bed? Does he put me first? Does he go the limit for me? Is he passionate? When he touches me, do I melt? Does he suck the lining out of my pussy? Is he a good provider and family man? Does he care about my wellbeing? Does he want me to be the best and have the best? Does he plan for our future? Does he even talk about our future? Do I bubble all over when I talk about him? These are the things that I need to answer and think about. Does this man talk about giving me the world? Has he ever told me that I am the best thing that ever happened to him?

Tomorrow, I will answer these questions. I'm going to sleep on them. Maybe, I need to re-evaluate my thinking and let this local joker go on about his long head.

November 12, 2006

This month has been hell. I had a really bad fight. My loans aren't closing at work, and he isn't helping the situation. One week he drinks, one week he doesn't. Flip Flop.

I was pregnant. The funny thing is, I didn't care. Right now, I'm in the wrong state of mind to have a baby. I'd like to have a baby after I'm married, but he doesn't want to get married right now. So, do I wait for something that might not happen or do I proceed on with my life? I've got to get a new job. Times are hard. I can't-do anything right. I feel like such a fuck up. But I won't fail. A few days later I had an abortion

December 16, 2006

Guess what, diary? This motherfucker called up some girl down South; one that he used to mess with. Now all of a sudden, we're getting phone calls and hang-ups. He claims he called to tell her about our wedding. What wedding?

Then check this out, this drunken fool crashed my brand new Saab into a city bus and kept going. He has to go. I hate him so much. I can't wait to pack his shit! This muthafucka needs AA. I'm not his savior. This muthafucka needs Jesus because Mohammad isn't helping him.

PS

God, please tell this mofo not to touch me no more. A nasty ass, stinky, alcoholic breath ass nigga. So not my style...garbage!

February 5, 2007

He lied to me about his whereabouts. He was in Texas for five weeks. I found out through a friend who he was with—his ex. It seems that she loves his dirty drawers, and I guess I have to face the reality that he cares about her too! This woman has been a thorn in my side for six years, and I'm tired of her. She told me that she would always talk to him and be his friend. Yeah OK! I told him before it's either her or me. I guess it's her. I've been wondering why he doesn't talk to me. Why there's no conversation…. just sleeping pills, snoring, and ignoring me. I need more. I deserve more. I'm hurt, but it takes a fool to learn that love doesn't love anybody. I'm not important, and I don't feel like I've ever been. I need to find a man who wants no other woman than me. I need a man who treats me like a Queen.

I can't get back all the lost time. It's gone forever. I need to smarten up. I've wasted so much time, but one day my husband and I will look back at this and laugh.

Ask CJ

Once you figure out who you are to be, you can never stop being that person.

This is something you need to think about: someone can use your weakness as a tool to destroy you. Of course, you must understand this isn't a good thing.

Never let anyone manipulate you into thinking that you can't live without them.

The puppet master uses a person's vices against them. Watch out for this.

The stories that women tell are far greater than the ones they tell silently to themselves.

You can see the cry for help in their eyes.

Women say that they want love, but when it is given, they don't know how to receive it due to the trauma of their past. We often have mistaken abuse for love. When a man hits you, he doesn't love you.

Mental, physical, sexual, verbal, and emotional abuse are all wrong and must not be tolerated by any woman.

The role of an abused woman is the greatest acting gig that has ever been scripted. It is far more than the apron that she wears to batter the chicken for her family's Sunday dinner and so much more than the lingerie she wears before the famous, "I came."

WOMAN, THE STRONGEST UTENSIL TO EVER BE USED:

A tear that drops from deception, abuse, and misuse is nothing more than a wet lie. Own your truth.

While in a toxic relationship we may feel ugly inside, but we put up a façade for the world. It makes us feel good to be desired, to have attention even if it's harmful or potentially deadly.

We do what we see and what we've been taught to accept.

What you see often you become accustomed to and not only accept but repeat.

A repeat offender.

There are many seasons in life that come and go, and sometimes you might have the same season more than once because you didn't get it the first time. To get through it; you have to remove yourself physically and emotionally from the situation. You can't wish your way out of it.

You can't be loyal to other people if you're not loyal to yourself. Be loyal to yourself by loving yourself first. Love yourself enough so that you will demand to be treated with the utmost respect. When people approach you they will immediately know if you have a high regard for yourself, "she thinks too much of herself." I had a man tell me that men usually look for women with low self-esteem especially at a club or bar. I said wow really but why? And he said because they are the easiest to take home and they don't require much.

 Grab hold of yourself, love yourself, and invest in yourself by becoming empowered. Take control of your life starting NOW!

Embrace who you are

Empower gives authority

Embark is to make a new start.

Who are you?

_____

_____

_____

_____

_____

_____

_____

_____

Who do you desire to be?

_____

_____

_____

_____

_____

The woman in the mirror is me. Past, present, and future. I will not run from her, be stagnant in her nor will I run to her, but I'll stand and embrace her and grow with her because I am that woman.

Don't Fix It! Don't Force It! Just Flush It! It is time for you to release the crap from your life. We all have some form of crap in our lives that we don't know what to do with. Crap comes in many different forms, and it can come from a variety of places. Sometimes we accept situations because we think we have to or simply because we don't know any better. Misinformed, misguided, and somewhat ignorant.

Not everyone needs to be a part of your life forever. We allow people to squat and take a nasty dump on us. God does not permit people to mistreat you. You allow people to mistreat you and abuse you. It's allowed behavior that starts within the self. The best part of a box of Cracker Jacks is the prize! Walk like you're the prize, talk like you're the prize, and make decisions like you're the prize.

Society has turned us into fixers. We spend the majority of our lives trying to fix relationships instead of letting SHIT go! We accept his shit, her shit, their shit, and a whole lot of bullshit! Eventually, you're full of shit, and that's called constipation. If you've ever been constipated, you are well aware that it's a miserable feeling. As I mentioned before;

We try to fix him because we don't want to be alone!

We try to fix him because we see the good in him!

We try to fix him because he's our kid's dad!

We try to fix him because the sex is good!

We try to fix him because he pays the bills!

We try to fix fix fix fix instead of flushing him and moving on

What did you get out of the experience? Learn from it and move on.

Let's look at this from a different viewpoint: unhealthy relationships can be toxic, and toxins are poisons that build up in your body and make you sick. Toxins can cause mental, physical, and emotional distress and in some instances, can even kill you. There has to be a detox to release the toxins from your body.

Low self-esteem reflects a person's overall emotional evaluation of their worth. It is a judgment of oneself as well as an attitude towards the self. Self-esteem encompasses beliefs about oneself (for example, "I am smart," "I am worthy"), as well as emotional states such as triumph, despair, pride, and shame. Smith and Mackie (2007) defined it by saying "The self-concept is what we think about the self; self-esteem, is the positive or negative evaluations of the self, as in how we feel about it." [1]

Low self-esteem comes from one's own self-doubt. A bad relationship will reinforce what is already in your mind. So, when we already have issues within ourselves, it's easy to allow the mistreatment from others. Allowed behavior is self-inflicted. Loving yourself is a required condition for building self-esteem. Boosting self-confidence and transforming a negative image of yourself into a positive image requires action, and that action is to fall in love with yourself before getting into any relationship. It is very hard to truly love someone else when you have no love for yourself. Self-love is the main ingredient in any good relationship. The moment that you decide that you don't love yourself, but you love someone else is the very moment that you give up your power. Power is a form of energy, and without power, your light is either out or very dim.

How do I fall in love with myself? Am I fulfilled? Am I happy? Are my needs met? What are my needs?

Overall Being

Basic human needs are the elements of human life and are common to all people. Our needs influence and drive our behaviors. If we don't get our immediate needs met, it affects our overall quality of life.

Let's take a closer look at how life should balance out.

1. Spiritual Being - Belief in there being greater than oneself.

2. Physical Being - the Basic need for food, shelter, exercise, water, air.

3. Intellectual Being - New thoughts, ability to learn.

4. Creative Being - Ability to express self through creativity.

5. Emotional Wellbeing - To have love, security, and respect.

6. Social Wellbeing- To have friendships and companionship.

Do you have a balanced life? If not what's missing?

_____

_____

_____

_____

_____

Here are a few questions that you can ask yourself

1. Am I allowing any form of abuse in my life? Physical, Mental, Emotional, or Sexual?

    _____

2. Do I take care of myself? Can I take care of myself if I leave?

    _____

Financially if I get out of this relationship can I take care of myself? How's my credit? What does my bank account look like? Do I have my own bank account? If you don't, open a small savings account now. How's my job stability?

_____

_____

_____

_____

Personal Hygiene: Am I clean? Do I bathe regularly? Do I comb my hair? Do I change clothes on a regular basis?

Health & Fitness: Have I let myself go? Have I traded in healthy choices of food for processed foods? Have I gained weight? Am I overweight? _____

3. Do I allow others to take advantage of me? Am I a walking doormat? Am I a "YES" person?

_____

_____

_____

_____

_____

_____

_____

4. Do I feel sorry for myself? WHY?

_____

_____

_____

_____

_____

_____

5. What do I think of myself? "I" is a key word here...

   What do "I" think of "MY-SELF?"

_____

_____

_____

_____

_____

_____

6. Who do I blame for my situation? Is this all my fault?

_____

_____

_____

---

7. Am I prepared to change? Am I ready for change?

Change starts in the mind. Your ability or inability to change starts in your brain. Until you change your way of thinking, you will always recycle your experiences. Instead of trying to fix situations, we need to fix our minds. When we fix our minds, situations will, in turn, fix themselves.

When we leave one relationship and go right into another one, it's called a "rebound" and what happens is we develop a false sense of love. Meaning we are not in love, but we'll go through the motions like we're in love but our hearts aren't truly in it....and we develop a false sense of love. Real love speaks volumes. Love is an action word. Love shows in your doing & giving. Being in love is not a one-way emotion it should be reciprocated.

Verbal Abuse

Verbal abuse can be as powerful and destructive as physical abuse and is much more difficult to identify.

- Criticism. You're never good enough. Harsh, persistent, and ongoing.
- Sarcasm. Cutting & throwing negative shade, aggressive tone, and nasty attitude.
- Put-downs. Repeated insults and attacks.
- Shaming. Disgust, you are horrible/wrong/fat, and nobody wants you
- Name-calling. Insults disguised as pet names, swearing.

Verbal abuse will make you feel insecure and doubt your self-worth. Verbal abuse tends to get worse with time. The longer you stay in a verbally abusive relationship, the more violent it will probably become. You've done nothing wrong so don't blame yourself. You have the right to have a healthy, happy, loving, and positive relationship.

"I Can Make You Love Me"

One night, I came home after working late to find my fiancée packing his clothes. I asked him what he was doing. He looked at me with a cold stare and said, "I don't like you. I don't like anything about you. I don't like the way you wear your hair... as a matter fact, I hate weaves, I don't like the makeup on your face, and I don't like the way you dress at all. Hell, I don't even love you."

Can you imagine someone saying these words to you after being in in a relationship with them for ten years? Can you imagine the pain that seared through my body when my fiancé gut-punched me with this? Can you imagine the breakdown of my mind, my soul, my entire being? Everything that I thought about myself was taken from me at gunpoint. I was robbed of my womanhood. I thought I was pretty; I thought I was sexy, I thought I had a good weave... But it wasn't just that, he said; "I don't love you or like you." I think that's the part that pierced every nerve in my body. I was numb, but as he attempted to leave, I fell to my knees screaming, crying, and begging him not to leave. He dragged me down the stairs as I held onto his Timberland boots. When we got outside, the ground was covered with snow as I ran behind him. I stepped on a broken bottle, but I didn't notice the snow turning red as I ran after him. Even though my flesh was hanging out the side of my foot, I ran after him.

I still wanted him; as a matter of fact, I wanted him even more. I wanted him so bad that I followed him to work, to his mom's house, to the barbershop and wherever I thought he would be. I would find the butts of Black & Mild cigars on the ground near his mom's house, and I'd wipe the dirt and debris from them and take them home and smoke them just to be near him to smell the essence of him. I would sit and cry all day and night. I stopped eating and began to drink alcohol profusely. I drank so much that I no longer had solid bowels. My bowels had liquefied. The rejection led me to a very sad and depressed state of mind. I wanted to kill him and had even planned it out in my head. I was losing it slowly… my mind.

The normalization of bad behavior is often derived from a dysfunctional upbringing and often considered normal because it's what we've seen. It's what we've become used to or what we're told is normal.

We become accustomed to abuse because it has been normalized—I have a black eye, and my mother had a black eye; I'm fighting with my boyfriend not with my husband, and I watched my mother do some of the same things with her boyfriends. As strange as it may seem, life has a way of repeating itself over and over and over again until we break the cycle of bad behavior until we break the cycle of generational curses.

We have to pull it up from the root. I'm talking about going into the pit, deep down into the stench of reoccurring bad choices and behaviors. We have to deal with the problems that are associated with abuse in our communities and what I've often seen, especially in urban communities, is that we will hide from our issues and cover them up rather than seek help. One of my exes fought me for years, but there wasn't a record of any of the incidences because I was programmed to believe that calling the police was for snitches and getting counseling was for crazy people... well, I was just that crazy.

➢ **Domestic Violence** – A violent or aggressive behavior within the home, typically involving the violent abuse of a spouse or partner usually with physical force.

➢ **Self-worth** – Respecting oneself while understanding and accepting one's strengths and weaknesses. Self-worth is often associated with feelings of inner strength, self-confidence, and the overall valuing of oneself.

➢ **Self-Actualization** – The understanding of self. A full realization of one's potential, and one's true self.

➢ **Emotional Intelligence** – According to Wikipedia, it is the capability of individuals to recognize their own and other people's emotions, to discern between different feelings and label them appropriately, to use emotional information to guide thinking and behavior, and to manage and/or adjust emotions to adapt to environments or achieve one's goals.

➢ **Emotional Self-Awareness** – Recognizing and understanding one's emotions and feelings with the ability to differentiate between them.

➢ **Common Sense** – Having sound judgment in simple situations.

➢ **Emotional Expression** – Openly expressing one's feelings verbally and non-verbally.

➢ **Assertiveness** – Confidence and forceful behavior. The ability to stand up for yourself.

105

➢ **Independence** – Being self-directed and free from emotional dependency on others. Decision-making, planning, and daily tasks are completed autonomously.

➢ **Problem Solving** – Finding solutions to problems in situations where emotions are involved. Problem-solving includes the ability to understand how emotions impact decision making.

➢ **Reality Testing** – The ability to see a situation for what it really is, rather than what one hopes or fears it might be.

➢ **Interpersonal Relationships** – Developing and maintaining mutually satisfying relationships that are characterized by trust and compassion.

Steps that you can take when you decide that it's time to Flush It!

1. Speak out! Tell family, friends or a ministry leader/mentor what's going on.

2. Start a savings account even if you only can save $5.00 a week. Skip the salon services sometimes and put that money away.

Pay off small bills and order a copy of your credit report. There are three major bureaus: Experian, Equifax, and Transunion.

Federal law allows you to get a free copy of your credit report every 12 months from each credit reporting company.

Online: www.AnnualCreditReport.com

Phone: 877 FACTACT

Did you know?

The Fair Credit Reporting Act (FCRA) entitles you to a free Credit Report under certain circumstances:

> ➤ Denied credit or you have experienced an adverse action.

> ➤ Victim of identity theft.

3. Start looking for a new place to live and secure it.

4. File a restraining order.

5. Change your phone number.

Emotional Detox:
Healing From the Inside Out

It's hard to heal when we don't take ownership for the now part of our lives. We often place the blame of life's negative occurrences on others. Often not able to establish who's really at fault for the things that we go through. It's easier to say it's her fault or his fault or their fault. Yes, genetics, as well as the general population that we grow up around, have a great deal to do with how we think, what we think and how we react to the behaviors of other human beings.

To heal is Forgiveness. Forgiving ourselves and then forgiving the other person to whom we felt has done us a disservice. So that I may forgive myself, I have to first apologize to myself. Apologizing to self-takes owning what is happening to me in the now season of my life. Was it my fault that I was abused, neglected or mistreated? No of course not it's never

109

your fault but when you allow it to continue you breathe life into the situation. You give it strength. Now it's time for you to be strong and let it go. All the pain, hurt and deceit. Give it back to the darkness that it came from. Invoke power into one's own life. Speak life and victory to yourself.

A scab may cover a wound or a cut, but it will still hurt if you press on it because it's still healing and healing takes time. Time does heal all wounds. Wounds have to be cleaned out first, you can't just bandage up or stitch up a wound or cut. Without proper cleansing and care you open yourself back up to infection (Toxins). Healing starts from the inside. An emotional detox will stimulate a mental recharge and much clarity.

Forgive Them & Yourself

Forgive yourself.

Apologize to yourself "I'm sorry for all that you've gone through, but from this day forward I'm going to do my best to protect you."

Invoke power from within yourself "There is a "SUPERNATURAL" being on the inside of you that's ready to emerge. Dig deep…

Time with yourself "Meditating and enjoying stillness with."

Heal yourself "I will speak positive affirmations to myself daily to encourage and solidify who I am."

F. A. I. T. H.

Daily Affirmations

I AM GREAT!

I AM WORTHY!

I AM STRONG!

I AM A LEADER!

I AM BEAUTIFUL!

I AM SEXY AS HELL!

I AM FEARFULLY & WONDERFULLY MADE!

I AM THE BEST AUTHENTIC VERSION OF ME, AND I WILL CONTINUE TO WALK INTO MY MOST EXCELLENT SELF!

Detox Bath & Cleanse

1. 1 cup of Epsom Salt
2. 1 cup of Baking Soda
3. ½ cup of Apple Cider Vinegar
4. ¼ cup of Castor Oil
5. Ten drops of Essential Oil
6. Shower Cap

Pour in salts and baking soda while the tub is being filled with water (hot to the touch). Slowly pour in remaining ingredients. Turn on inspirational music I prefer soaking music which can be easily found using Pandora or YouTube. Put a shower cap on to help increase sweating. Sweating is your body's way of getting rid of toxins. Relax and clear your mind, lay back and allow your body to release all negativity.

My 21 Day Internal Detox

Nothing white!
No candy, cakes, cookies, crackers, chips!
No soda or high fructose juice!
No dairy!
No sugar!
No flour!
No red meat or fried food!

Enjoy fresh fruits, vegetables and drink smoothies for 21 days.
Allow your digestive system to take a much-needed break.
Drink herbal teas and lots of alkaline water.

Consult with your doctor before detoxing or dieting.

Resources

The National Domestic Violence Hotline

1800-799-7233

Info for Survivors of Domestic Violence Rape Abuse

Incest National Network

1-800-656-4673

The National Teen Dating Abuse Helpline

1-866-331-9474, TTY 866-331-8453

Or online chat

www.loveisrespect.org

Rape, Abuse & Incest National Network Hotline

1-800-656-HOPE (4673)

www.rainn.org

www.online.rainn.org

Suicide Prevention Hotline

1-800-273-TALK (8255)

http://www.suicidepreventionlifeline.org

There is a significant chance that you or someone you love could be affected by domestic violence. More than 1 in 3 women (35.6%) and more than 1 in 4 men (28.5%) in the United States have experienced rape, physical violence and stalking by an intimate partner in their lifetime. Physical abuse includes physical assault, battery, and sexual assault used as part of a systematic pattern of power and control perpetrated by one intimate partner against another. Physical abuse can cause severe injury and even death. It often co-occurs with other forms of abuse, including psychological abuse, economic abuse, and stalking. Psychological abuse involves trauma to the victim caused by verbal abuse, acts, threats of acts, or coercive tactics. Perpetrators use psychological abuse to control, terrorize, and denigrate their victims. It frequently occurs before or concurrently with physical or sexual abuse. Economic abuse is when an abuser takes control of or limits access to shared or individual assets or limits the current or future earning potential of the victim as a strategy of power and control. In economic abuse, the abuser separates the victim from their own resources, rights, and choices, isolating the victim financially and creating a forced dependency for the victim and other family members. (NCADV.ORG)

THE FACE OF TOXIC PEOPLE

Dr. CJ Hornes is a happily married mother of 4 who lives in Atlanta, Georgia with her wonderful husband of 6 years Rodney Hornes.

A very special thank you to my raw, uncut, tell it like it is aunt "Farrah" who told me, "Lisa flush that shit" I love you, and I was listening.

I once had these as regrets, but now I am more thankful that my experiences have gone beyond regrets and become a point of reference for others to learn from.

----Lisa